Piano

For Itzhak Perlman

Theme From

"SABRINA"

From the Paramount Motion Picture SABRINA

For Solo Violin and Piano

JOHN WILLIAMS

ISBN 978-0-7935-9861-8

Visit Hal Leonard Online at
www.halleonard.com

HAL•LEONARD®
CORPORATION
7777 W. BLUEMOUND RD. P.O. BOX 13819 MILWAUKEE, WI 53213

for Itzhak Perlman
Theme From "SABRINA"
From the Paramount Motion Picture SABRINA

JOHN WILLIAMS

Solo Violin

For Itzhak Perlman

Theme From

"SABRINA"

From the Paramount Motion Picture SABRINA

For Solo Violin and Piano

J O H N   W I L L I A M S

ISBN 978-0-7935-9861-8

Visit Hal Leonard Online at
www.halleonard.com

HAL•LEONARD®
CORPORATION
7777 W. BLUEMOUND RD. P.O. BOX 13819 MILWAUKEE, WI 53213

for Itzhak Perlman
Theme From "SABRINA"
From the Paramount Motion Picture SABRINA

SOLO VIOLIN

JOHN WILLIAMS